DEBBIE PAGE-WOOD

The Panty Thief

The Adventures of Pringles

To those who knew Pringles,
may he always be remembered.

Pringles
Beloved Catty
February 2007 – 29/04/2020

Contents

1

The Adoption

I've always been a cat person. Growing up we didn't have pets, but our neighbour had two cats and two dogs. The cats would come over for cuddles and playtime most days. I couldn't wait until I was old enough to live alone and get my own cat.

I was sixteen and spending the weekend at a friend's house, Julie and I were sitting in the warm Autumn sun on her driveway, laughing and chatting, when her neighbour's one-eyed ginger cat sauntered over for some love and affection.

It was love at first sight. I knew I wanted a ginger cat one day. There's just something about ginger kitties that makes me all mushy inside.

Fast forward thirteen years. I'm twenty-nine, and my long-term boyfriend, Gary, and I recently bought our first apartment: a three bedroom flat in Durban, overlooking the rugby stadium and out to sea.

It's a Friday afternoon and I'm sitting at my desk in Kingsmead Office Park during my lunch break, browsing through the online noticeboard, when pictures of a handsome ginger kitty catch my eye.

"Pringles needs a home," the listing says, giving contact details for a lady called Rose.

Immediately, I email a copy to Gary, 'Look how cute this kitty is. Please can we get him? Please.'

A few minutes later his response arrives, 'Phone and see if he's still up for adoption.'

Tentatively, I dial the number, preparing myself to be disappointed.

'Yes, Pringles is still looking for a home,' Rose replies.

Excitedly, I arrange a date with her for me to meet both her and Pringles.

The following week, on a Tuesday afternoon, I drove from the cricket grounds to her house on the Bluff. My heart pounding in my chest, excitement rising with each passing kilometre, I couldn't wait to meet this furry bundle. Arriving at her address, I parked the car and knocked on the door.

'Hi, I'm Debbie,' I said, smiling, as Rose introduced herself.

'Come on in. Pringles is around, somewhere,' Rose said, leading me through their hallway into the bright, sunny lounge. My eyes scan the room for any sign of ginger fur, while Rose starts asking me questions.

'Have you had a cat before?'

'No,' I respond truthfully, 'but my neighbours had cats, and I've house sat for people with cats before.'

'We haven't had much interest in Pringles and we need to find a loving home for him soon.'

'Do you mind if I ask why?'

'We're emigrating and can't afford to take all our animals with. We're sad to be parting with him, and would really like him to go to a loving home.'

'It must be hard having to choose which of your fur kids to keep and which ones to give up,' I replied, putting myself in her shoes for a minute.

I don't think I'd be able to do it.

'Oh, look!' I exclaim. 'He's curled up inside the dog kennel.'

Rose comes over to the ranch slider, 'Let me get him for you.'

Carrying the ginger bundle inside, Rose puts him down and lets him wander around. Pringles immediately jumps up onto the coffee table.

That's not going to happen in my house. I don't want cat hair on my dining room table or kitchen counters.

Rose disappears into the kitchen and returns with a snack for Pringles.

'Pringles,' she calls, holding out a piece of ham and handing me a little piece. I crouch down, holding it out. Tentatively, he comes over, sniffing furiously, wanting the ham but unsure of the person holding it. I keep as still as I can. Slowly, he creeps closer before gently pulling the meat from my fingers.

'Can I pick him up?' I ask.

'Of course.'

I scooped him up and gently rub his ears. A purr rumbles through his little body and he lifts his chin to be scratched underneath.

'How old is he?' I ask, curious.

'About eighteen months. We're not one hundred percent sure, but he was born sometime around February 2007. He was found in the bush behind our property, along with his siblings. They were only a few weeks old and had to be hand reared and bottle fed. The other kittens were all adopted out once weaned, but we kept Pringles.'

'Has he been vaccinated, neutered and microchipped?' I ask.

'Not yet.'

'I'd love to adopt him.' It was love at first sight. I need this gorgeous kitty to be part of my life. I have so much love to give him. 'Would it be possible for you to have him neutered and vaccinated? I'll pay to have him microchipped.'

I knew I couldn't afford to get all of it done, and Pringles should have been neutered and vaccinated before he turned a year old.

We made arrangements for Rose to drop him off at their vet on Friday morning, and I'd pick him up Friday afternoon after work. It would give Rose and her family time to say their goodbyes, and Pringles would still be slightly anaesthetised from the procedure. I was hoping he wouldn't remember the drive home. I wanted to prevent him trying to run back to the Bluff.

Three days later, Rose dropped Pringles off and I knew I'd be collecting him in a few hours. The day couldn't pass quickly enough.

I arrived at the vet clinic and collected one very wobbly, very sleepy ginger kitty.

'Could I get his vaccination booklet?' I asked the vet.

'Sorry, he hasn't been vaccinated. We only microchipped and neutered him,' he replied.

'No problem. I'll get that done next week.'

I carried my precious bundle out to the car. He slept for the entire forty-five minute drive home. We arrived and I opened the cat carrier, Pringles wobbled out on unsteady legs. Taking one look around the strange room, turned and went back inside the cat carrier. I left him sleeping there with the gate open.

An hour later, he slowly emerged, exploring the room in a low, slow, slinky creep before I picked him up to show him where his litter box and food bowls are. Placing him gently on the floor next to his water, he sniffed at it before creeping back into the lounge, hiding behind one of the curtains.

Worried that he might be in pain, I folded up a soft blanket and placed it underneath him, pulling the curtain around him once more. He seemed to feel safe behind it. Refusing to eat or drink, Pringles slept on the blanket in the corner of the lounge for the next three hours with me checking on him every half hour.

Later that night, I scooped up my new kitty and gently carried him through to the bedroom, laying him down in his soft bed, right next to ours. He didn't stay there long, as soon as the lights were off, he hopped up onto my bed so I put my arm out and he curled his little body up against mine, snuggling into my armpit, resting his little head on my shoulder and we fell asleep together.

Our first night together was strange. Gary was away, competing in the Fish River Canoe Marathon, and I wasn't sure what to do with Pringles. I had no idea if he knew how to use a litter box, and being an ex-feral, I thought he might be used to doing his business in the garden. I had a restless night's sleep, waking up every couple of hours to check on him.

Is he still breathing? Does he need to drink? Does he need to use the litter box?

I was worried about the side effects of the anaesthetic and gently carried him over to his water bowl, trying to coax him to drink with no luck. He refused and we snuggled up together on the bed, again. I dozed off and woke up a little while later. The warm furry body was gone. I listened, and in the stillness of the early morning I heard little lapping sounds, Pringles was finally drinking. Relief flooded through my body. He was going to be okay. A few hours later he used his litter box.

Pringles was recovering from his operation. Time for his adventures to begin.

2

Sprinkles

The apartment we live in is built at the base of a slope, so the first floor is at street level with pedestrian walkway entering the building adjacent to our front door. This gives Pringles easy access to the garden from the entrance foyer, all he needs to do is follow the short corridor from our apartment to the garden. He wants nothing to do with it. We've had him for a week and he's still refusing to go outside. If I pick him up and put him in the corridor with me, he runs inside and hides under the bed or behind a curtain.

I've nicknamed Pringles 'Catty', a combination of the words cat and kitty, and he loves to sit on the sunny lounge window sill and look out over the communal garden, watching the birds, often twitching his whiskers and making funny little chirping meows almost as if he's daring them to come closer.

Sitting on the couch, reading, mid-morning on a Saturday a strange movement catches my eye. I look up in time to see Pringles's furry bum and tail disappear off the window ledge. My heart hits my stomach. I feel sick. I can't believe he's just jumped. It's about five and a half metres onto the grass below. If we'd been on the ground floor, it wouldn't have been a problem, but it's a long way down. Scared that he's injured himself, I tentatively look out the window, only to see Pringles trying to come home the same way he got down.

The silly sausage is fine, although clearly scared about being in the great outdoors.

Shoving my feet into a pair of shoes and quickly unlocking the security gate, I run down the flight of stairs as fast as my legs will go. I get onto the grass, but Pringles is gone. I look around.

Where could he be?

Standing under our window, I look up.

No, he couldn't have climbed up there. Could he?

I look straight ahead, into our downstairs neighbour's lounge window and see him standing on the back of their couch looking at me.

Unfortunately – or fortunately, depending which way you look at it – our neighbours are out. Running back up the stairs, I grab his bag of catnip and a bag of kitty treats before returning to the garden.

'Pringles, treats,' I call, shaking the bags, trying to coax him out the window. 'Come on, Catty. Fishy, fishy, fishy.'

It takes me half an hour to finally coax him out through the window, finally jumping out onto the grass and greeting me with purrs and leg rubs. I give him a few treats before carrying him upstairs.

'You silly cat. What were you thinking? You could have hurt yourself,' I scold him.

I still have one problem to deal with – how am I going to explain the sandy cat paw prints on my downstairs neighbour's internal window sill? I've never met them before and don't want to just leave it. I feel bad that my cat made a mess inside their home.

I'm not sure how long they'll be out for, or if they've gone away for the weekend, and not knowing when I'll see them next, I decide to write a little note. I leave the note in their mailbox, along with a photo of Pringles, apologising for the mess and explaining what happened. I finally see our neighbours a week later and apologise in person. Thankfully, they're very understanding, saying that it's not a problem.

Over the following months their little daughter, Riley, and her friend, Keira, who lives a few doors down, become good friends with Pringles. I often come home from work to find one or both little girls waiting for me outside my garage.

'Can we feed Sprinkles?' they ask.

'His name is Pringles, and yes, you can feed him.'

Following me up the stairs, they wait patiently while I measure out his biscuits, arguing over who had fed him last and who gets to do it today.

I'd already started Pringles's training, thinking I could train him the same way people train their dogs.

'Fishy, fishy, fishy,' I call and Pringles comes running. 'Sit.'

He sits on command and one of the girls places his biscuits in his bowl. They both bend down and stroke him while he eats, making him purr.

Riley and Keira never stay long, they just wanted to feed and touch the cat.

Sometimes I'll be hanging laundry and they'll ask where the orange cat is hiding.

'We want to play with him.'

'Catty,' I call, only to have him leap out of a bush or emerge from a hiding place under the building, his sudden appearance giving the girls the giggles. I'd leave the girls to play with him and Pringles soon went from being a cat who didn't like too much attention, to being one to sought out any love and scratches he could get.

It didn't matter how many times I told the girls that his name was Pringles, they'd always giggle and insist on calling him Sprinkles. So, Sprinkles it was, and they continued to call him that for the next five years.

Things were great for a few months and I decided to split Pringles's daily food portion into three to stop him from guzzling it all down in one go, choosing to feed him half in the morning before I left for work, a quarter when I got home, and the last quarter at bedtime. I'd often arrive home from work to find him sitting in the corridor outside our flat, like he knew it was dinner time, or he'd be waiting with the girls at the garage and would lead us up.

After his great flying leap out of the lounge window, we soon realized my Catty was a rascal; not only did he get up to mischief during the day while we were at work, he insisted on keeping us up at night, too.

For the first six weeks he woke us up every single night, at least three to four times, meowing for no apparent reason. He'd wander around the flat in the dark and then stand in the middle of the passage, usually outside our bedroom door and meow loudly until one of us called out to him. After the first two weeks, we began to feel the same way new parents must feel - extremely tired and horribly sleep deprived. Thankfully, the sleepless nights eventually eased when Catty finally settled down and adjusted to his new home and daily routine.

3

Colic, Bladder Infections, Depression and Acne

Being a domesticated feral, Pringles's skin seems to be thicker than a normal domestic cat's skin and the vet often struggles to administer his injections.

The very first time I took Catty in for his annual vaccinations I noticed the vet having difficulty getting the needle in.

'Is he a feral?' he asked.

'Yes, he was found as a kitten, hand-reared and bottle fed. Why?'

'Sometimes ferals can have tougher skin. You might want to look away if you're squeamish,' he said before stabbing the vaccination needle into Catty's neck, the thick skin of his scruff making a little popping sound. Catty didn't even notice and I soon became used to this rather violent application of his injections.

I think Catty softened up over the years, as his vaccinations became less violent as he got older.

Just after Pringles's second birthday, I woke up one morning to find him refusing food and water. Not wanting to eat was unusual for him, he'd always finish his biscuits in one go, but today he was lethargic, his little tummy bloated and swollen.

I phoned the vet and made an emergency appointment before bundling Pringles up into his kitty carrier and driving him over. The vet examined him, looking in his mouth, checking his teeth, and feeling his tummy.

'He's developed a bad case of colic,' the vet informed me. 'Has he eaten anything strange lately?'

'He has been eating geckoes,' I replied. 'We often find the back legs on the doormat. There was one there this morning.'

'Hmm. There is a particular type of South African gecko that can cause colic if they eat the head. Does he eat the whole thing?'

'Everything except the back legs and bum,' I replied.

How am I going to stop him from hunting geckoes and eating the heads?

Pringles, now an outdoor kitty, has reached a stage where he dislikes being locked inside. He much prefers spending his time in the garden. If we do lock him in he gets stressed out, so it's easier to let him come and go through an open kitchen window.

I really didn't have to worry. After suffering for a week, Pringles seemed to learn from his mistake and was much more selective about what he ate. We'd often find what we came to call "tops 'n tails" left on the doormat. He'd eat the body of the gecko, leaving the head and front legs, back legs and tail stump.

At least he was avoiding things that made him sick, but this was not the end of Pringles's medical troubles. I didn't know it yet, but I was about to start spending a lot of time at the vet.

Most ginger cats are male, with a few, rare, ginger females. The problem with male gingers is that they're prone to developing crystals in their urine, which can cause recurring bladder infections. Pringles was no exception.

He developed his first bladder infection at the age of three. In less than two months he had three more flare-ups, numerous visits to the vet, medication, and lots of tender loving care. After the third flare-up the vet suggested we put him on prescription cat food to help prevent the build up of these crystals. The expensive new food seemed to help, but he'd still have an odd flare-up or infection over the coming years.

Pringles came and went as he pleased through the kitchen window, having free reign of the communal garden. The children in the apartment block would play with him during the day while I was at work, and I'd have playtime with him every evening and on weekends, especially on laundry days.

Unfortunately, stress from his recent bout of cystitis, numerous vet visits and all the medication had obviously taken their toll on his little body, and my poor Catty became horribly depressed. It got so bad he wasn't eating, would hardly drink, and he didn't even want to play any more, not even with his favourite toy. Back to the vet we went.

Catty was examined before being put onto anti-depressant tablets. I needed to administer these three times a day for two weeks and this meant having to drive home from work during my lunch breaks to medicate him. Of course, my work colleagues and friends thought it was hilarious and they teased me endlessly about having a cat with depression. I didn't think it was funny, but how many cats do you know of that have been depressed?

I don't think I'll ever live it down. To this day, people still don't believe me when I say cats can suffer from depression.

After finishing his course of anti-depressants, Pringles was back to his usual, playful self. We finally have the bladder infections under control and were hoping that this was the last of our expensive vet bills.

And then he got acne.

Just like any teenager, Pringles developed acne on his chin. It looked like a rash of tiny little yellow pimples and blackheads. I tried so hard to figure out what was causing them. First we tried different foods. Nothing changed. Then I started cleaning under his chin after each meal, but that didn't seem to help. After lots of trial and error, there was only one thing left to try; I changed his water bowl from plastic to stainless steel.

All his food bowls are all stainless steel, and you won't believe it, his acne cleared up within a week. After having battled with his acne for almost four months, I never would have guessed something as simple as a plastic water bowl would be the cause of a reaction like this.

I could finally scratch my Catty under his chin once more.

4

The Panty Thief

Pringles went through something that we call his "nesting phase" - he'd bring home dried leaves and palm fronds, dragging them in through the kitchen window before putting them on the floor and meowing at us to come see what he'd brought.

One day, our neighbour saw him doing this and asked if he was building a nest. We had a good chuckle and it became something that Pringles did.

Until the night he upgraded from leaves.

I heard Pringles coming in through the window, heard the thump of him jumping from the windowsill to the floor, and got up to see what he'd brought in. I was expecting a leaf, not a tiny pair of tan corduroy shorts. There was only one family in the apartment block with a little boy under the age of two, so I knew exactly who they belonged to.

Returning the shorts the following morning, Pringles followed me downstairs. I was feeling rather sheepish as I knocked on their door.

'Good morning,' I greeted when the door opened. 'I think

these belong to your little boy,' I said, holding up the shorts.

'Oh, yes. I wondered where those got to,' she replied.

'My cat brought them home,' I explained, pointing to the furry offender winding around my legs.

She laughed, 'They must have fallen out my wash basket when I brought the laundry in. Thank you for returning them.'

'No problem.'

I saw a little face peeking out from behind her legs.

'Hello, would you like to pat the kitty?' I asked him, crouching down. The little boy nodded. I picked up Pringles, holding him in my arms as the little boy approached slowly. 'Gently,' I said, as he put a hand out to touch the soft fur.

'Orange,' he replied, looking up at me.

'Yes, he's an orange cat.'

From that day on, the little boy would always ask where the 'orange cat' was whenever he saw me. I had to keep an eye on them whenever they were in the garden together, though. Sometimes the little boy's pats would become a little too rough and Pringles had a tendency to nip if he didn't like it.

A few days later, Pringles brought home a rag. I had no idea who it belonged to or where he'd gotten it from.

Had it come off the washing line? Did he take it from someone's garage or apartment?

I picked it up and carried the rag downstairs to peg it onto the wash line for the rightful owner to claim.

The following week, Pringles upgraded once more. This time bringing home a pair of brand new Woolworths ladies boy short panties. They still had the cardboard tags and price attached. I had no idea who they belonged to so I hung them up on the communal wash line, hoping the owner would find them.

The next night Pringles brought home another pair - same brand, same style, same size, with the tags still on - just a different colour and pattern. This time I pinned the underwear to the communal noticeboard in the foyer with a note. The previous pair was still hanging outside on the line.

When Pringles appeared the next evening with a third pair of panties, I knew I had to do something. Showing him the offending item, I told him in a stern voice that he was a 'bad cat' hoping he'd get the message.

Somewhere out there was a poor woman missing three pairs of brand new underwear, quite possibly from inside her locked apartment. I could only imagine what was going through her mind.

If it was me, I'd be wondering where my underwear was disappearing to, how, and if I had a stalker. Just imagine discovering your underwear missing without any signs of an intruder.

When the fourth pair arrived at 7pm the following evening, I knew telling Pringles that he was a bad cat hadn't worked. I picked up the latest pair of undies and went to see if I could find the owner in our apartment block. I walked up and down the corridor, knocking on every apartment door that had a window or door open - somewhere he could have possibly gained access - and asked if the underwear belonged to anyone living there, explaining the situation and that this was now the fourth pair.

My not-so-innocent Catty was happily trotting along next to me, almost as if he was proud of what he'd done, and curious to see if I could solve the mystery.

My little tale brought forth many chuckles and a few exclamations of, "Oh, he's so cute!" whenever Catty popped his head around my legs to see who I was talking to.

No one admitted to owning the underwear.

I began to wonder where in the neighbourhood he was getting them from, and just how far he was roaming. I could just picture Catty merrily trotting down the side walk, a pair of panties dangling from his mouth, front legs having to swing sideways as he trots home. It must be an extremely funny sight to see.

Over the following two nights, two more pairs of these panties appear. Whoever this lady is, she's now missing six pairs of brand new underwear.

I kept the underwear in a paper bag in our laundry, in case I ever discovered the owner.

I never did. A few months later, the six pairs of underwear were donated to a local charity shop, tags still intact.

5

African Adventures

I can't remember if it was our second or third Christmas with Pringles, but we woke up around 3am to a loud tinkling crash. Thinking we were being burgled, we crept through the apartment - Gary armed with his bōjitsu stick, me with a can of deodorant, which stings if sprayed in the eyes.

Turning on the lounge light, we discover our Christmas tree on the floor, baubles and tinsel scattered everywhere, and Pringles's head sticking out of the middle of the tree, his eyes as big as saucers, his tail fully fluffed and as thick as my forearm.

I couldn't help but laugh.

My silly sausage had decided to climb the plastic Christmas tree and as he neared the top, it became top heavy, causing cat, tree and baubles to come crashing down.

Needless to say, darling Catty never attempted to climb a Christmas tree again, but he does love to sleep underneath one.

Four years after getting Pringles we had to install a cat flap. Catty had always used the kitchen window to get in an out, but after an attempted break-in at 2am, the cat flap became a necessity.

We hadn't even had the flap a week when we were rudely awoken around 5am by very loud meowing and yowling. Thinking there was a cat fight going on in our lounge, we padded through the house, my heart pounding in my chest, my hair standing on end, only to find Catty lying outside on the doormat, his front paw trapped in the cat flap.

Pringles had been playing with the swing door, swatting it as if it were a toy, and somehow managed to get his paw well and truly wedged between the bottom of the clear perspex flap and white plastic frame. The front paw was upturned, the flap wedged in between the soft little paw pads, and there was a lot of wiggling, pulling, pushing, and struggling going on while we tried to free him.

Twenty minutes later, just as we were contemplating breaking the perspex flap, his paw simply popped out. I don't know if Catty finally relaxed enough to let his paw splay, or if he moved at just the right angle, but he was finally free.

Unfortunately, he didn't learn his lesson. The same thing happened a second time, a month later, also in the early hours of the morning.

Being an ex-feral, Catty loves to hunt and will hunt anything that moves, from grasshoppers, lizards and butterflies, to the occasional bird - although bird hunting is severely discouraged - and even your feet if he's in the mood.

Being on the rather "festively plump" side, it's more often a miss when it comes to stalking birds. Most of the time I manage to make a noise and chase the bird away before he gets too close. In the five years that we've had him, he's only caught three birds, all of which were brought to us very gently, as unharmed gifts, and we're able to rescue them and set them free.

WARNING: blood and murder mentioned in the next paragraph.

One morning, I woke up, got dressed for work, and padded through the apartment to have breakfast. Walking into the lounge, I put the light on only to be greeted by what looked like a murder scene. There was a large pool of deep scarlet blood splattered across the carpet and scattering of grey feathers everywhere. Pringles had managed to catch a sleepy pigeon in the early hours of the morning and decided that this one was not going to be a gift – he was going to eat it for breakfast.

Having to clean pigeon blood and feathers out of a hand woven cream coloured mohair carpet at 6am is not fun. Pringles knew he was in trouble and made himself very scarce.

I never knew that much blood could come from one little bird.

There's one adventure of Pringles's that I'll never forget.

I came home from work to find him playing with something on the grass in the front garden. Thinking that it was just an insect, a cricket, or a lizard, I left him to it.

Halfway up the staircase to our apartment, I could see Catty shaking his front paw violently with a long, thin, bright green thing dangling off it.

A snake!

Dropping my handbag on the staircase, I kicked off my high heels, and completely ignoring my phobia of snakes, ran down the stairs and across the grassy area in my stockinged feet to rescue my Catty.

Meanwhile, Pringles had become irritated with this thing that was biting his paw and he proceeded to pounce on the snake's body. By the time I reached Catty, he'd bitten the snake a few times and it had let go of his paw.

My heart pounding, I scooped Pringles up, leaving the snake on the grass. Running upstairs with tears streaming down my face, I hysterically shouted, 'Gary! Gary! Catty's been bitten by a snake, he's going to die!'

'What kind of snake was it?' Gary calmly replied.

'I don't know. Pringles bit it, it looks dead. It's downstairs on the grass.'

'Are you sure it's dead and hasn't slithered off?'

'I don't know. I'm more worried about getting Catty to the vet.'

In my mind, a snake is a snake, they're all poisonous as far as I'm concerned. I wasn't going to hang around to see if it was dead. Walking outside, Gary goes downstairs to have a look, with Catty and I trailing sheepishly behind him.

It turns out it was only a harmless bush snake, and yes, it was dead. Pringles broke its neck when he bit it and there was no need to take Pringles to the vet.

6

The Land of the Long White Cloud

We moved halfway around the world in July 2013, from Durban, South Africa to Auckland, New Zealand. We chose to bring Pringles with us. Many people told me I was crazy - yes, it was expensive, but I couldn't bear the thought of having to leave my fur kid behind. Pringles is part of our family.

The poor little guy went through a lot with the move: he was put into a cattery for a month before we flew out so that relevant vaccinations, inoculations and paperwork could be done. I also didn't want him around while we packed up the apartment as I was trying to reduce his stress levels as much as possible.

He also needed vet visits, fortnightly, for rabies inoculations and signing of additional paperwork by a state vet, and there are only two state vets in South Africa, one in Johannesburg and one in Cape Town. It made sense for me to use a pet travel agent and have him booked into their cattery in Cape Town. They took care of all the necessary arrangements and paperwork, made sure Pringles was put onto his flight, and they liaised with MPI quarantine in New Zealand.

The day we left South Africa, Pringles flew on a different airline to us. He flew with Quantas from Cape Town to Auckland, via Sydney, a 20-hour flight, while we flew Durban to Johannesburg, before departing for Auckland via Dubai and Melbourne, a 32-hour flight with Qatar Airways. We chose the longer flight to get 30kgs of luggage each, which we needed, as this was all we'd have with us until our shipping container arrived ten weeks later. This also meant Pringles landed in Auckland a day before us.

The pet travel agent had arranged for someone from the quarantine facility to pick Catty up from the airport, and he was placed directly into quarantine for ten days, and we weren't allowed to visit him during that time.

When I was finally allowed to collect him, I hadn't seen him for six weeks. We arrived at the quarantine facility and were taken through to see Pringles. He was sleeping in his quarantine cage.

'Pringles,' I called, but got no response. 'Pringles,' I tried again. Still nothing. 'Catty?' Not even an ear twitch of recognition. I was hurt.

Has my Catty forgotten me already? Or is this payback for all that he's just been through?

I walked around his cage, opened the gate, and put my hand in to stroke his soft fur. It was the end of July - mid-winter - and bitterly cold. The quarantine facility had spoilt him, they'd put an electric blanket inside his kitty bed and he was so toasty and warm that he didn't want to move, let alone come home. Coming from a Durban winter where the average winter temperature is between 16°C and 25°C, Pringles had never had to grow a winter coat before and he was really feeling the 8°C cold.

We were staying with Gary's aunt and uncle until we could find a place to rent, and a few days later I went to Bed, Bath and Beyond to buy Pringles a fleecy baby blanket as I kept finding a 'mole tunnel' in our bed - Catty would burrow his way up from the bottom of the bed, underneath the duvet, before lying with his head on my pillow and the duvet covering his body. This was not on. I didn't want to sleep on a pillow full of cat fur.

Once he had his fleecy blanket, he happily slept under it for hours on end.

While staying with Gary's aunt and uncle, we kept Catty locked inside 'our' bedroom, just in case he decided to make a run for it. We needed to get a few groceries and left the bedroom window cracked open ever so slightly to let some fresh air in. I had done this before as the windows are quite stiff - I even battle to push them open - and I thought Pringles would be fine.

I forgot to mention that Pringles is petrified of a vacuum cleaner. His fear of the vacuum started shortly after we got him: Catty had been hiding behind a curtain and I hadn't seen him there. As usual I vacuumed the carpet before running the vacuum under the curtain, where I accidentally sucked up Pringles's tail. The poor cat must have thought the vacuum was trying to eat him. As soon as I realised what had happened, I turned it off, releasing his tail, but all I saw was an orange streak darting for the door and out into the garden.

Well, Catty must have heard the noise of Gary's aunt starting up the vacuum and in a frantic panic, with super-catty strength, he managed to force the stiff window open wide enough to escape. Out into the unknown New Zealand wild he went.

We arrived back to discover Pringles missing. My heart sank. I'd just brought him all this way, only to have him disappear without a trace into Albany Reserve.

I called frantically, walking up and down the fence line, listening in case he meowed in response, but all I could hear were Tūīs and Eastern Rosellas in the bushes. We called and hunted for a good fifteen minutes before Gary found him hiding underneath the house, directly below the window he'd escaped through. Thankfully, Catty hadn't gone far.

It took a while to coax him out with Gary crawling into the small space to get him, and we never made the same mistake twice – we always made sure the window and door were securely closed before going out again.

We'd been in New Zealand for just over three and a half weeks when we found a townhouse to rent in West Harbour near the marina. We signed the paperwork, paid the deposit and first month's rent, and moved in the next morning. Promptly packing up the car with borrowed linen, our luggage and the cat – the shipping container with all our household goods and clothing was still in transit, all we had were the two suitcases we'd flown over with – so we were able to fit everything into the car and could do the move in one trip. It was about a twenty kilometre drive, so off we went.

After having recently been in a cattery for a month, flown for hours inside a noisy air plane, being locked in a quarantine facility cage, and now being inside the cat carrier again must have stressed Pringles out immensely. Not even three kilometres down the road, he 'dropped one.' It was a cold, grey, rainy day and, thankfully, I'd put newspaper down in his carrier. We ended up having to drive the next seventeen kilometres gagging on the smell with our windows rolled down and the rain coming in.

It wasn't funny at the time, but we laugh about it now.

After that little incident, we were hoping our first night in the new house would be unadventurous. What wishful thinking! A strange house with strange smells, and there'd been another cat living here before we moved in.

Pringles kept scratching at the doors and windows trying to get out. It continued for at least half an hour and in desperation - Gary had to work the next day and needed sleep - we ended up putting Catty in the laundry room with his food, water, litter box and bed. It was the only contained area with a tiled floor far enough away from our bedroom. We woke abruptly at 5am with a loud bang.

I crept downstairs to see what was going on. Pringles was jumping up and hanging onto the door handle in an attempt to open the laundry room door. Whenever he let go, the handle would flick back up, and the loud bang we heard was Pringles falling against the washing machine. Somehow he managed to slide the barrel bolt across, effectively locking himself inside.

I panicked.

How are we going to get him out?

The door handle unscrews but both sides need to be accessed to do this, and there are no visible screws on the outside. Gary came downstairs.

'What's going on?'

'Pringles has locked himself in and I can't get him out,' I cried.

'Stupid cat. Give me a minute.'

Fetching one of the dining room chairs, Gary carried it through the inter-leading door to the garage, and that was when I remembered the louvre windows. We'd left the top set open so Pringles would have fresh air.

There we were, at 5.30am, Gary standing on the chair to reach the top louvres, slowly reaching in and sliding the next set of louvres out their frames, handing them to me to carefully place on the ground before getting to the handles on the lower ones to open them and do the same. Twenty minutes later, the louvres had been painstakingly removed and there was now a space big enough for Gary to climb though.

He unbolted the door and let himself and Pringles out. Hugging Gary and thanking him, I began replacing the windows.

Needless to say, Gary wasn't very impressed with the cat.

A few weeks later, we woke to the hair-raising screams of a catfight. It's two in the morning and sounds like it's taking place in our lounge.

That's odd, I'm sure I locked the cat flap.

Slowly creeping down the stairs, torch in hand, the hair on my neck standing on end, I was ready to break up a cat fight. Reaching the last step, I feel for the light switch before stepping down onto the carpet, expecting to see fur everywhere. There's none.

I look around and see Pringles's tail sticking out from under the curtain next to his cat flap. Thinking the other cat must be sitting on the deck, I turn on the outside light and whip my half of the curtains open. Nothing.

Pringles growls. I turn the outside light off to try see what he's seeing, only to find my darling pussycat has been having a full on yowling match with his own reflection. The heavy blackout curtains and bright street lights created the perfect reflection.

Silly cat.

Pringles, Catty, Sprinkles, Orange Cat, Thunder cat - the townhouse has wooden floors and he loves the sound his paws make when he goes tearing down the staircase, especially at night - whatever his current nickname may be, he drives us nuts, has us in fits of laughter, and can be extremely entertaining.

We love him to bits and cannot imagine our lives without him. I'm really glad we chose to bring him with us when we moved.

7

Funny Stuff

When we still lived in South Africa, we only had one next door neighbour as our apartment was at the end of the corridor, right next to the staircase. She had two cats; a fluffy long-haired Persian called Misty and a younger grey short hair called Kimber.

Misty was a real madam with serious cattitude - she'd walk around like she ruled the place. Over the months Misty taught Pringles a few bad habits, along with some of her cattitude rubbing off on him. One of these bad habits was to flick his tail. Whenever he was upset or was told off for being naughty, he'd flick his tail up and down quite violently, almost like he was flipping us off. It was very cheeky and yet so funny.

Misty's 'little sister', Kimber, was an extremely shy but very sweet kitty. We hardly ever saw her, but on the odd occasion we'd find her curled up on our doormat in the sun with Pringles. As soon as Kimber and Pringles noticed that someone had seen them, they'd get up and saunter off in opposite directions, as if they didn't like each other.

This little 'love affair' of theirs went on for years, either taking place on our doormat or the neighbours' doormat, with the cats always pretending they hadn't been curled up together whenever they saw a human.

Pringles loves fish - any fish - fish flavoured cat food, tuna, fresh fish, you name it, usually the stinkier the better. His biscuits are fish flavoured and he gets fresh fish scraps whenever Gary goes fishing.

Gary's parents came out to South Africa for a visit in 2009, and his dad left a can of pilchards in tomato sauce in our grocery cupboard when they left. Neither of us eat pilchards so I had a thought.

Why not wash the tomato sauce off and give the fish to Pringles over a few days?

It seemed like a good idea and the fish wouldn't go to waste.

Two days into this fishy treat, and Catty was absolutely loving it. I was sitting in our home office organising the seating chart for our upcoming wedding, when Pringles ambled in and fell asleep under my chair. A few minutes later, I hear this high-pitched, squeaky noise emanating from under the table, accompanied by an awful fishy stench. I gagged and had to leave the room, opening the windows. I picked up the can of air freshener and gave the apartment a good spray.

Pilchard cat farts are the worst! I will never feed Catty pilchards again.

A few months before we moved to New Zealand, Pringles brought me a gift.

He dropped it in the communal corridor outside out apartment and did his deep 'rowr' for me to come look. I walked outside and immediately started laughing.

'You naughty cat. Who's pork sausage have you stolen?' I

asked him. 'Gary, come look, the silly sausage has actually brought a sausage home.'

As I turned and looked back down, the 'sausage' grew legs and started running off down the corridor. I squealed.

'Gary, come quick! The sausage is running away!'

He came out to have a look. 'That's not a sausage, that's a shrew.'

For those of you who don't know what a shrew is, it's a little South African rodent. They're usually nocturnal and eat insects, spiders, earthworms and millipedes. This one must have been a juvenile as it was the size, shape, and colour of a cooked pork sausage, except it had little ears, a pointy nose and a tiny tail, all of which I didn't see at first.

'Don't touch it,' Gary warned. 'They've got sharp teeth and they bite.'

He went inside to fetch his thick D.I.Y. gloves, while I kept an eye on both the shrew and Catty. Gary gently picked the shrew up and I had a closer look. It was quite cute.

Gary carried it out to the garden, putting it under a bush and it immediately started to burrow. I don't know how or where Catty found it, but he was locked inside for the rest of the afternoon until we were sure he'd forgotten all about the shrew.

The rental townhouse in West Harbour has a cat flap set into the floor-to-ceiling window next to the ranch slider. The flap has a much more simple design than the one we had in South Africa, but Pringles can't seem to figure out how to use it. I don't know if it's because the entire the flap is clear and cats mainly see in shades of grey, but trying to teach Pringles how to use the cat flap was becoming really frustrating.

If I let him out through the front door and closed it, he'd

happily come in through the cat flap, but he refused to exit the house through it. The silly sausage would just sit there and scratch at the window, waiting for someone to either open a door or hold the cat flap open before leaping through it.

I spent an entire Saturday afternoon with him using his toy mouse as bait. I played with the mouse, poking it through the cat flap, and even left it sticking half in and half out. Pringles swatted at it, knocking it outside and I left him to figure out how to get his mousey back. We did this a few times until he realised he could stick his paw through the flap from the inside. The next day he went out all by himself.

Catty has free reign of the townhouse's small garden during the day, but we lock him inside at night. Cats are creatures of habit and after two weeks of living in New Zealand, he got used to having the cat flap locked around sunset. Once settled into this routine, he began coming in on his own as soon as it started getting dark, curling up in his little bed and settling down for the night. As soon as our alarm goes off in the morning, he makes a beeline for the cat flap, waiting to be let out.

One chilly winter's evening, we were sitting watching television, Pringles curled up in his kitty bed near my feet, his soft baby blanket draped over him, covering both him and the bed completely. We call this a Catty Pie. Soft snoring noises along with little grunts and squeaks emanate from the depths of the 'pie', when all of a sudden Catty shoots out of his bed, straight up in the air, reaching a height of about one metre before landing on all four paws and immediately leaping straight into the air again.

Sitting on the floor next to his bed, looking dazed and confused, Catty glances at his bed, looks at me, and looks at his bed again. We couldn't help but laugh. Of course, this made Pringles act all sheepish - he hates being laughed at.

The poor little guy must have been having a nightmare. It was so funny, it looked like he was on a trampoline. I wish we'd had enough warning to capture it on camera.

We still laugh about it, years later.

It's 2015, and we've just bought a house in Whangaparāoa. Gary is doing yoga in the lounge, as he'd done many times before, but there must have been something about this particular headstand that Catty didn't like. His hackles rose, his tail went all floofy and he hissed loudly at Gary before hastily slinking off, dragging his gut on the ground, to hide under our bed.

To this day we still have no idea what was so scary. Pringles has never reacted to a headstand like that again.

Fast forward to February 2020.

It's early on a weekday morning and we're in the kitchen making breakfast. Pringles is usually sitting at his bowl waiting for biscuits, or winding around our feet asking to be let out, but he's no where to be found.

'Have you fed Catty and let him out already?' I ask Gary.

'No.'

'Have you seen him?'

'No.'

'Me, either.'

I hunt all over, checking under beds and couches, behind curtains, and in all his usual hiding places, but he's simply vanished. Knowing its not possible as I'd locked him in the night before, it was hard to believe he was just gone.

Where could he be?

I walked over to the cat flap to check I'd definitely locked it the night before, only to discover that my little Houdini had pulled the entire locking mechanism out of the device, letting himself out.

And so my morning began.

I phoned our local Animates store in Silverdale, where we'd bought the microchip cat flap.

'Hi, my name is Debbie,' I said to the customer services department. 'I have an unusual request. I'm not sure if I need to speak to you, or to someone in your pet department.'

'I can try help,' she replied. 'What's your query?'

'We bought a SureFlap microchip cat flap from Animates a few months back, and my cat has managed to pull the locking mechanism out. I'm phoning to see if you sell replacement parts, or if you know where I could get one from.'

'If it's come out, you simply need to push it back in. It should still work.'

'I tried that, but he's cracked one of the little plastic arms. It doesn't stay in, it just pops back out and is very loose.'

There's a giggle on the other end of the line.

'I'm so sorry, I didn't mean to laugh,' she says, 'but I just have this mental image of a cat pulling the lock out.' There's more laughter. 'Let me transfer you to our pet department and see if they can help.'

I get transferred, only to have to repeat the entire conversation again.

'I'm so sorry, but this is just hilarious,' the lady in the pet department says to me. 'In all the years I've been working here, I've never heard a story like this. We don't sell spare parts, but I do have a box of spares lying around from damaged or faulty cat flaps. Give me a minute, I'll rummage through it.'

I'm trying hard not to laugh because I can just imagine how funny this must sound to these strangers. I'm starting to develop images in my mind of Pringles with his teeth on the locking mechanism, front and back paws bracing, while he pulls with all his might.

Who would have thought a cat would break out of his own home?

'I'm so sorry, we don't seem to have anything. You might want to try contacting the manufacturers.'

I thank her and hang up. Pulling out the manual and warranty, I dial the 0800 number listed, only to have to repeat my tale for a third time. Once again, the sales consultant has a good chuckle. After giving her the serial number she says she can send us a replacement part for free, as it's still under warranty.

Sometimes it's really hard to explain to strangers exactly what my ginger ninja gets up to.

Shortly after getting off the phone with the SureFlap consultant, Pringles saunters into the conservatory and lies down on the mat, looking at me as if to say, 'I didn't break your expensive cat flap. I found it that way.'

8

Cat 'Flu

In May 2015 we flew back to South Africa for three weeks to attend a family wedding, visit friends, and do a bit of sightseeing. We found a cattery with good reviews in nearby Greenhithe and booked Pringles in for the month.

Upon our return, we collected him only to receive a warning that they'd had a few sneezing cats the week before.

'Keep an eye on Pringles in case it's cat 'flu,' she warned me as we were leaving.

Cat 'flu is highly contagious and the cattery should have been quarantining suspiciously ill cats away from the rest. I have no idea if they did this or not.

We got Catty home that afternoon and he seemed fine. He was very happy to be home, full of purrs, and constantly wanting love, to be scratched and patted. He did have the odd sneeze, but it wasn't enough for me to be worried.

The next day he sneezed a lot and I began to think something was wrong. Being a Saturday afternoon, the vet had already closed for the day, so I had to wait until Monday to speak to someone. I didn't think a few sneezes warranted calling the expensive emergency vet. Catty still sounded fine.

Pringles kept us up that entire night and by Sunday evening he had a runny nose accompanied by loud sneezing fits with five or six continuous sneezes.

By Monday morning, he was so blocked up that he had to breathe through his mouth. He was sleeping on the bed with me and woke me up throughout the night with his sneezing, coughing and sniffling. He refused to eat breakfast or drink any water, so I rushed him off to the vet as soon as I could, only to be told that he had the dreaded cat 'flu.

There are three types of cat 'flu: one viral that doesn't respond to antibiotics, and two bacterial types that can be treated with antibiotics.

Pringles has the horrible viral kind, the one that cats can die from it if not treated in time. The poor little guy is running a high fever of 40.8°C. Normal for a cat is around 38°C. We're lucky that the 'flu is still limited to his nose and throat and hasn't gone into his chest yet. We caught it early.

The vet gave Pringles painkillers, and an antibiotic injection to prevent him getting a secondary bacterial infection. I paid my hefty bill and took my sick Catty home.

Tucking him up into his bed in the weak winter sun, and covering him with his baby blanket, I feel helpless. There isn't much I can do to help him, he just has to fight this off on his own.

Dosing Pringles daily with painkillers, as well as a precaution-ary antibiotic, I also give him half an L-Lysine tablet crushed and added to his food. Viral cat 'flu causes cold sore-like blisters on the soft palate in the mouth, inside the nasal cavities, and in the throat, and L-Lysine can help inhibit this. It's no wonder my poor Catty doesn't want to eat.

After force-feeding him food and water with a syringe for two days, he finally 'asked' for breakfast on the third morning and a great sense of relief washed over me.

His health was slowly improving and I could finally medicate him in his food, without having to use the syringe.

Poor Pringles sounds awful. He has to be locked inside as it's June - the beginning of winter - and there's a chilly wind blowing. I have to try prevent him from developing a further infection, like pneumonia, or from infecting any neighbourhood cats.

Placing his bed next to the locked ranch slider in a sunny spot, I tuck him up, thankful that my little furry bundle is happy to let his body rest. He sleeps for most of the day, and it's now a case of waiting it out.

Poor Catty's nose is so badly blocked he can barely breathe, but it keeps running. If he isn't trying to breathe through his mouth - which cats hate to do - then he's trying to breathe through his nose, which causes him to constantly sniff, sneeze and cough.

The vet said it can take anything from three to fourteen days for his symptoms to clear, and I feel so sorry for Pringles. There isn't much I can do to alleviate his symptoms, other than 'steaming' him twice a day.

In the morning, I run hot water in the shower until the bathroom is all steamy - just like you do when a child has croup - before carrying Catty into the bathroom. I stand holding him in the steam for a few minutes, until his breathing eases a little and he starts expressing mucous when he sneezes.

At night, I put him in the bathroom with me. He sits breathing in the steam by himself, and seems to realise that this is helping him, as he happily follows either of us into the bathroom.

Just when we thought Catty was getting better, we had another set-back.

Pringles refused to eat or drink. After trying to get him to eat by himself, with no luck, I had to resort to force-feeding with the syringe. This time he was not tolerating it. He growled at me, squirmed and scratched my arms. I had liquidised cat food everywhere. I was getting irritated and he was clearly frustrated.

I'd syringe fed him when the cat 'flu first flared up, but he must have felt really miserable then, because feeding was a breeze, he just lay there and lapped it up.

I gave up trying to feed him and had my own breakfast.

'It's easy and very simple to force-feed him his medications in a syringe,' the vet had said. 'Just mix a teaspoon of wet food with a teaspoon of water and add his medications. Put the 10ml mixture into a syringe and simply trickle it into his mouth.'

Clearly this vet has never tried to force-feed an ex-feral with a syringe.

An hour later, I tried again. Catty still wasn't happy, but reluctantly let me feed him his medication mixed with food. Not even five minutes later, Pringles decided he was hungry and went and sat by his food bowl.

Why won't he just eat his medications and get the rest of his food afterwards without all the fuss? Sometimes it's like having a naughty toddler in the house.

I hate having to force-feed him, but I know it's only helping him. In his eyes, I must be this big, bad meanie trying to shove unwanted stuff down his throat.

His blocked nose sounds awful, but his fever has finally broken, and I can feel his body and ears aren't nearly as hot.

What really irritates me about this whole episode is how blasé the cattery has been. When I phoned, they spoke to me as if it wasn't a big deal. Cat 'flu is serious! It really worries me that the carrier or sick cat may still be in the cattery, not quarantined away from other people's pets. One thing I know for sure, I'm never taking Pringles back there.

It's so hard to describe how awful he looks and sounds. He's lost 500g, which is not a lot to most people, but to a 6.5kg cat, it's a lot. To try give you an idea of what my poor kitty sounds like, it's as bad as a human adult with a really bad case of the 'flu without being able to blow his or her nose.

After a lot of frustration with the latest force-feeding episode, I happened to read the flavour on the critical care food tin the vet had given me - chicken and pork - and my fussy cat doesn't like eating anything that isn't fish flavoured.

This could explain why he hasn't wanted to eat. If I mix his medications with fish flavoured cat food, would he happily eat it?

I drove to the vet and asked if I could swap all remaining unopened tins for fish flavoured, and it worked. After three days of force-feeding, Catty happily ate his medication all by himself.

All this unnecessary stress for nothing just because his food didn't taste like fish.

Pringles was seriously ill with this 'flu. After nearly two weeks of tender loving care, he slowly started coming right. He began to eat on his own and sleep through the night, but it took nearly four months for him to recover fully.

There were definitely times when it was touch-and-go. At it's worst, we thought we were going to lose him.

Unfortunately, the virus is now in his body for life. As soon as he gets a little stressed, it'll flare up and he'll start sneezing. The cat 'flu virus remains dormant in the body in the same way that the cold sore or herpes simplex virus does in humans.

Giving Pringles half an L–Lysine tablet crushed in his food whenever he starts sneezing seems to help to suppress the virus, and so far, we haven't had another bout of cat 'flu.

I truly hope we never have to go through that again.

9

A House of His Own

We moved from the rented townhouse in December 2015, when we bought a free-standing house with a large garden on the edge of Whangaparāoa golf course. Pringles hated being locked inside for the first week after we moved. He just wanted to get out and hide under the house. We kept him locked in for a week, just to be safe. I didn't want him running away or getting lost, and we let him out a few days before Christmas.

Pringles likes to think he's rough and tough, but he's definitely a "Mommy's boy," and often comes off second-best when fighting other cats. More often than not, he'll be the one who starts the fight. His favourite trick is to yowl and meow until I go out to investigate, only to have him hide behind my legs as if to say, 'Ha! I've got back-up.'

I'm usually armed with a tumbler of water to toss on the unwanted visitor - it's the easiest way to break up a cat fight without getting scratched to pieces - and neither kitty gets harmed.

Our house has a rainwater tank and we're not connected to

council water supply. I woke up early one morning, just before sunrise during our first week in the house, with Pringles yowling, 'Mom! Mom!' It's his rescue me meow that sounds exactly like a small child calling for his or her mom.

Armed with a torch and a tumbler of water – it was still dark outside – I crept down the staircase before tiptoeing along the path leading around the water tank. I wasn't sure what I was expecting to find, but there was Pringles, perched on top of the large concrete water tank with the offending cat crouching on the ground. As soon as Pringles saw me he got all brave, leaping off the tank and chasing the trespasser across the lawn, down the garden and over the back fence onto the golf course. The cat took off home and Pringles hopped back into our garden, strutting towards me as if to say, 'Did you see, Mom? Did you see? I chased him!'

I've never seen that cat in our garden again, but its really funny how Pringles seems to need backup before taking action.

Pringles and I were at the bottom of the garden one morning – I was taking photos of the recent changes we'd made – when a fluffy white cat suddenly popped out of the thick belt of agapanthus bordering our property. Without thinking I hissed at it, letting it know it wasn't welcome in its own language, hoping it would turn and run home. Instead, it bounded out the bushes and took off at a sprint up towards our house. Catty took off after it, both cats running flat out, as fast as their little legs could go, fur looking sleek in the breeze.

A very brief cat fight took place under the house before Pringles flushed the white cat out onto the driveway. With Catty circling from one side, I positioned myself on the other, effectively cornering this unwelcome visitor.

Or so we thought.

Before I knew it, a white streak zoomed past me, around the side of the house and simply disappeared. I wasn't sure which way it had gone. The poor thing must have been terrified, though, as there was a strong smell of cat pee near our laundry steps. I looked over at my poor Catty. The hair on his body standing on end, his tail puffed up as large as my forearm. Even his whiskers and eyebrow hairs had turned curly. I've never seen a cat's whiskers and eyebrows go curly before. I didn't know they could.

I picked him up and gave him a cuddle before carrying him inside for a treat. As soon as he calmed down, his whiskers and eyebrows straightened out again.

We never saw the white cat again.

10

Adopted Grandparents

Not long after we moved to Whangaparāoa, Pringles decided that our garden wasn't big enough and he took to roaming our adjacent neighbour's gardens, unaware that the neighbour on the right already had a 'groundskeeper'.

Pringles came leaping over the 6ft wooden fence as fast as he could go, his tail all puffed up, eyes as big as saucers. We assume that Linton's little Australian terrier had snuck up on him while he was exploring the garden, and even though we'd been told the dog is 'cat-friendly', Pringles must have been caught unawares. Usually, he'll stand up to a dog if he feels the dog is in 'his' territory, but ever since that morning he's only roamed our garden and the neighbour's on the left - Murray and Joy's place.

Murray and Joy say they don't mind, and Pringles is often found lying in a sunny spot at the bottom of their garden, supervising their gardening, or overseeing odd jobs.

Pringles loves attention and will often seek it out, especially if he hears a group of voices outside. There have been mornings where he's been lying peacefully at my feet, only to suddenly dash out of the cat flap to see who has arrived to visit Murray and Joy.

He's even followed a door-to-door salesman from our house to theirs, just like a dog, and I've noticed when I go out during the day, Pringles waits a few minutes before hopping over the low fence to go next door for a cuddle. He loves to sit on their windowsill, sunning himself. He's never done this with any of our neighbours in the past and we've never encouraged it, but he's adopted Murray and Joy as part of his extended family. At least I know where to look for him when he's not home. It comforts me to know he's got company if I'm out for the day, or busy with clients. I don't mind having a 'timeshare' kitty, as we all get to enjoy his company, and it seems to have prevented him from wandering the neighbourhood.

We still lock Pringles in at night, purely for his safety and my peace-of-mind. Our house is on a busy main road and locking him in has drastically reduced the number of cat fights he gets into, as most seem to happen at night.

Catty seems very happy and is still playful for his ten years.

I warned Murray and Joy shortly after we moved in that Pringles is a cat-burglar, telling them about his panty thieving days. It was almost as if Catty heard us talking, because a few days later he brought home a rag.

I returned it to Murray that afternoon, but the following morning the rag was back. This backwards and forwards game with the cloth continued for a week until Murray finally knotted it to the railing next to their garage where my little rascal couldn't pull it free. Don't get me wrong, he tried.

I saw him through our kitchen window having a tug-of-war with the cloth. Holding it in his teeth, little furry body tugging and pulling with all his might, and the railing not giving up the cloth.

Stealing Murray's rags eventually turned into a game of hunting garden gloves. After visiting Joy one afternoon, Catty came home with both her gloves, which he promptly deposited at the base of our staircase, meowing deeply for me to come see what he'd brought. I assumed they were Joy's and immediately took them back. She was still working in her beautiful rose garden when I walked across, Pringles trotting along after me.

'Hello,' I called out. 'I believe these belong to you?'

Joy looked surprised and glanced around, looking for her gloves.

'I had them a minute ago. I took them off to briefly attend to something else.'

'My little rascal ran off with them and brought them home.'

We both had a good chuckle. Clearly Pringles had seen his opportunity to do a grab and dash.

The game of bringing me gifts has never gotten old. The most Pringles has ever brought in one day was three rags: first a dishcloth, then a face cloth, and finally a hand towel.

Some of the weirdest things he's ever brought me were a shrew, the six pairs of panties, and a banana peel from Joy's compost bin.

A week after he stole Joy's gloves, Catty started tossing my garden gloves out the repurposed shower rack that I have hanging near my gardening tools. Pringles can reach it if he stands on the water tank.

We'd been doing some major repairs after our basement flooded (this was April 2017) when an ex-tropical cyclone hit Whangaparāoa, causing slips and flooding in the neighbourhood. Pringles clearly thought we weren't paying him enough attention and used my gloves as a means to communicate this. I always put them in the same place, yet was constantly finding them scattered along the footpath, or one in the garden and another on the staircase, or both hidden on top of the water tank.

Maybe he likes that they get returned to the same place each time? Maybe it's his kitty version of Hide-and-Seek?

Pringles loves chasing leaves in the garden, even more so if I drag a cabbage tree leaf around for him to pounce on. He also likes to play Hide-and-Seek, usually with me hiding and him seeking - he stalks me before pouncing and then runs away while I hide again. Sometimes he hides, but he's not very good at it - there's always a tummy or a tail giving his hiding spot away.

And he loves to play tag. We do this either in the garden or inside. I'll tap him gently on his rump and then run away. He'll turn, running after me before tapping my ankle or leg with one of his paws before turning around and running off, waiting for me to chase and 'tag' him again. Sometimes a game will go on for a good twenty minutes with us chasing each other around the garden.

I've often wondered what other neighbours and the people on the golf course must think? Crazy cat lady?

11

Creepy Crawlies

We got to use the wood burner for the first time during winter in Whangaparāoa. We'd never had one before and Pringles had no idea what it was. It went from being extremely scary with him hiding under the bed every time we put firewood on, to it being tolerated from across the lounge, to finally becoming his favourite thing.

By the end of winter, Pringles couldn't seem to get close enough. On days when it wasn't cold enough for a fire, he'd sit in front of it, giving us disgusted looks as if to say, "Where's the warm?"

One morning, Pringles woke me up shortly after Gary had left for work. It was early, somewhere around 6am, and still dark. Catty was sitting on the carpet in the bedroom making his deep, guttural 'rowr', which usually signals that he's brought me a present. Still half asleep, I thought that Gary might have forgotten to open Catty's cat flap, but it was only when he made the deep-throated 'rowr' once more that I realised he'd brought something inside.

Turning on the bedroom light, I half blinded myself, battling to focus on the large insect on the carpet. At first glance, I thought it was a huge spider. The hairs on my arms and back of my neck standing on end, my heart racing, I wondered how I was going to pick this thing up ... And then I saw feelers moving.

Holy heck, that's a giant cockroach, my brain screamed at me.

I had another look, my eyes still not fully focusing in the bright light.

Okay, that's not a cockroach. It looks more like a cricket on steroids.

I finally recognised it for what it was - a wētā. For those of you who don't know what a New Zealand Wētā looks like, its sort of like a cross between a cricket and a locust - this one was around 6cm long, with spiky legs, a long ovipositor (a female) and large mandibles.

This was the first wētā I'd ever seen up close and just wanted to get it outside before it crawled into a cupboard. I'm not sure if it was a ground wētā or tree wētā, I just grabbed a tissue and picked it up, walking through to the lounge to get to a window above the garden as fast as possible. This thing was giving me a serious case of the heebie-jeebies.

Halfway across the lounge floor, it wriggled and I dropped it. Why I hadn't just opened the ranch slider in the bedroom, I'll never know. Fumbling for the light switch in the early dawn light, hoping I wouldn't step on the wētā in my bare feet, I finally got the light on only to discover it had simply vanished.

I knew it was impossible for something that big to just disappear into thin air. I dropped it mere seconds ago on an open carpeted area.

Where could it be?

I hunted everywhere - looking under furniture, on the carpet, on the walls, doors and curtains - but it was gone. Taking a few steps backwards, one of my pyjama pant legs felt weird. I glanced down, and there it was, clinging tightly onto the fabric just above my ankle.

Eek!

I tried to pull it off, but it refused to let go. I tried again.

It's not working. How am I going to get it off me?

I got goosebumps from head to foot and my skin started crawling. Finally, the wētā let go. I ran to the window and placed it on the external windowsill. The last I saw of it, it was crawling along the side of the house directly above the garden, fully intact and completely unharmed. I'd managed to rescue it before Catty decided he wanted it back.

We've learned over the years when Pringles brings a gift, it's usually caught, carried, and delivered very gently. Nine times out of ten it's unharmed when we get it. If I'm going to rescue it, I have to move fast, otherwise Catty changes his mind and starts playing with it, or he delivers a fatal nip meaning he's going to eat it, possibly leaving a nice mess on the carpet.

12

Splish! Splash!

At eleven, Pringles is still as playful and mischievous as ever. He loves getting in the shower after someone's finished, to drink the warm water on the shower floor.

Why? Nobody knows. He has a water bowl that's filled daily with fresh, clean water.

One downside is that he hasn't learnt to wipe his little paws when he's done, leaving a trail of wet kitty paw prints across the bathroom floor. Sometimes there's a soggy tummy and tail print, too, if he's decided to sit for a while.

One afternoon, Gary was doing some D.I.Y work and climbed into the shower to wash off the grime. Pringles decided to join him, perfectly happy standing under the warm shower spray. By the time they got out, Catty's fur was soggy and he contentedly stood still while I dried him off.

I find it so weird that he meows for me to dry him if he gets wet when it's raining, but he'll happily stand in the shower. Maybe he likes that the water's warm?

We had a really bad thunderstorm a few months later - Pringles is petrified of thunder and usually hides under the house or under our bed at the first grumble in the distance. On this occasion, the storm moved in really fast and the first clap of thunder came out of nowhere. Catty must have been lurking at the bottom of the garden with the only hiding place nearby being a large drainage ditch running between our property and the golf course.

Preferring to lock Catty inside during a storm, I called and called, but there was no sign of him. I started to worry. Pulling on gumboots and a raincoat, I checked all his usual hiding spots, but couldn't find him anywhere. Rain was bucketing down, lightning followed closely by loud claps of thunder. The storm directly above us.

Almost an hour later, the storm passed and an extremely dirty Catty came slinking in through the cat flap. He was filthy: sopping wet and coated with mud from his shoulders to the tip of his tail. Only his head and shoulders were still ginger, the rest of him was a dark, muddy brown with leaves, twigs and other debris sticking in his fur.

I tried to dry him with a towel, but mud and water kept dripping everywhere, sticks and leaves not budging, and his fur feeling dirty and cold.

'I'm going to have to put him in the shower and wash all this muck off,' I said to Gary, not sure if I was going to be scratched to pieces.

With only one bathroom and no bath, the shower was the only option. I ran the water until it felt warm, turned it off, and placed Pringles on the shower floor. I was worried it was going to be difficult holding him with one hand, operating the shower head with the other. With the shower door open, me kneeling on the bathmat, and Pringles standing in the shower, I turned the water on gently and started to rinse him off.

He just stood there.

The poor little guy looked so cold and scared that I don't think he cared what was happening. He knew he was safe and inside. With all the muck and debris finally off, I wrapped him in a fluffy towel and cuddled him, trying to get as much water out his fur as I could. Setting him down gently on the lounge floor in a patch of weak sun, I brushed him before leaving him to lick himself dry.

For nearly fifteen minutes he had this really dazed look on his face, almost as if to say, 'What on earth just happened?'

In hindsight, I wish I'd thought to snap a photo of him before putting him in the shower. To be honest, I was more concerned about getting him warm and dry as quickly as possible, photos were the last thing on my mind. I can only guess that he was hiding in the ditch, facing the same way as the water flows, meaning water and debris flowed over him in the opposite direction to the way his fur lies. It would explain how all the debris got truly wedged in there.

Our bath mats started looking a bit worn and tired so I ordered plush polyester ones from The Warehouse. I bought two: one for outside the shower and one for the base of the vanity, hoping that Pringles would walk over the mats after being in the shower to dry off his paws. He walked over the old one, but it wasn't very absorbent any more, and these new ones felt so much better. I actually thought he'd prefer the feel of these plush ones, as they're similar to the inside of his kitty bed - which he loves - but the new bath mats are lava! Pringles refuses to step on them.

If I lay them out in a way that there's no option but for him to stand on one, he squirms around, trying to figure out how he won't have to touch it. It's hilarious.

Two weeks later, we were getting ready to go to bed and Pringles followed us into the bathroom while we brushed our teeth. I explained to Gary what I wanted to do and went to fetch Catty's bag of treats while Gary laid both bath mats on the floor, blocking the doorway. We wanted to see if we could get Pringles to finally walk on them.

I pulled out my phone and turned the video on, coaxing Catty to come to me with the cat treats. Pringles still didn't want to step on the mat. I placed a trail of cat snacks on the carpet, but the mats were still 'lava.' He wasn't going near them. He wiggled and squirmed, wanting the snacks but trying to figure out how to get over without making contact.

Wiggle, squirm, wiggle, squirm, wiggle ... Finally, he did a huge, awkward leap, clearing both mats and landing on the carpet.

Catty 1, bathmats 0. Snacks achieved.

He's such a silly sausage.

Pringles loves drinking out of the bases of pot plant pots, dirty puddles, and rainwater collection bins. He seems to prefer these dirtier water options to the nice clean water he's given daily. His latest favourite drinking spot is the bird bath.

Yes, he perches himself on the side of the birdbath, like a big furry bird and proceeds to lap up the water, especially if I've just scrubbed it clean. He knows he's not allowed to chase birds, we've discourage him as part of his training with 'Uh uh' or 'Leave it', so this must be the next best thing.

13

Winky the One-Eyed Pirate

Pringles was in a nasty cat fight about a year and a half before we emigrated. He was scratched across his left eye, and at the time I had our Vet check him out only to be told permanent damage had been done and there would be a little on-going inflammation in the future. I was given eye drops to put in Catty's eye whenever he seemed uncomfortable, or if the eye oozed, and we were sent home.

Slowly, his left eye started to look darker than the right. Instead of having two yellow eyes, he now had one yellow, and one spotted with brown freckles. I took him back to the Vet to make sure he still had sight in both eyes. Before emigrating, I took him to a feline eye specialist for a second opinion. She informed me that his eyesight was fine, although issued a warning he may gradually go blind in that eye as he gets older.

Pringles battled with cystitis and bladder infections from the age of three. Crystals forming in urine is common with ginger cats, and was something we had to monitor and treat with prescription cat food. We'd been through so many bouts of cystitis that I could tell if Pringles was starting with a flare-up, and would begin medicating him immediately to prevent a blockage. One peculiar side-effect of the anti-inflammatories causes Catty to hallucinate. He sits in the middle of the lounge watching imaginary things flying around - we call it 'seeing pink elephants.'

His most recent bout of cystitis happened in June (2018). I bundled him into his cat carrier and took him off to the Vet, expecting it to be a routine visit with more medication.

The Vet walked into the consultation room, took one look at Pringles and exclaimed, 'Oh, my! Look at your eye. You poor cat.'

'I'm sorry? I don't understand. I'm here to have his cystitis treated. What's wrong with his eye?' I asked, shocked by her reaction. I explained the prior cat fight, the previous vet and eye specialist's diagnoses, and had a copy of the report in Pringles's file. 'I know the brown colour of that eye is due to inflammation. When it flares up the eye gets weepy and I have drops to put in.'

'I'm sorry to tell you it's not just inflammation. Pringles has developed a case of sudden onset glaucoma. His eye is swollen, hard, and is probably putting pressure on his brain causing him migraine-like headaches.'

Sadly, cats don't show when they're in pain. I had no idea this had happened.

'I feel awful. I should have brought him in sooner.'

'Don't feel bad, there's no way you could have known,' the vet replies.

I was given two options: an operation to remove his eye, or to medicate him with eye drops, twice a day, for the rest of his life.

Do I end up with a one-eyed cat? Or do I medicate him daily? Which would be best for him?

I couldn't help it, I burst into tears right there in the consultation room.

This is all too sudden. I'm here to have Catty treated for cystitis, only to be told he needs an eye removed.

I got the medication for his cystitis, plus the eye drops I would have to put in his eye twice a day for a week before surgery if we choose to go that route. I paid and took my Catty home.

I let him out his cat carrier and walked next door. Gary was still at work in the city, and I needed someone to talk to. Knocking on Murray and Joy's front door, I felt like an emotional wreck. Joy opened the door and I burst into tears.

'I'm so sorry,' I said tearfully.

'What's wrong, Deb?' she asked, rubbing my forearm gently

'Catty needs an operation. He's going to lose his eye,' I sobbed.

Joy wrapped me in a hug, rubbing my back gently and whispering soothing words in my ear about how I couldn't have known and that it wasn't my fault.

I cried for twenty-four hours, not because Pringles had to lose an eye, but because I felt like an awful person for not realising he'd gone blind in that eye.

The fact that it happened gradually meant we never saw any change in Pringles's daily routine, behaviour, or playtime. It was also why he never walked into furniture - he'd had time to adjust, slowly.

I still felt awful.

We made the decision to have his injured eye removed. It would give him a better quality of life - he'd be pain-free and wouldn't have any unnecessary stress from eye drops being administered daily.

A week and a half later, I dropped Pringles off at the Vet Clinic.

They'd be keeping him for the day.

He had his operation and his eyelids were stitched shut. I'd been given the option of having a prosthetic ball inserted under the eyelids, for aesthetic purposes, at extra cost. I chose not to do it. I knew once the wound had healed and the fur grew back, the sunken eye socket would hardly be noticeable. I didn't want to add anything that could possibly cause issues later on.

I collected Pringles later that afternoon, and the vet nurse warned me he wasn't happy about wearing a "cone of shame" - he'd been pulling it off all afternoon.

I was now the owner of a one-eyed fur kid.

'I recommend securing it with a cat collar,' the nurse said as we left.

We got home and I put his collar on, but even that didn't work. He wriggled and pulled until he got both the collar and cone off. I had an idea. I'd bought a body harness with leash so I could take him into the garden when he had cystitis - I needed to monitor if and when he was peeing, and how much, without him running off. I secured the cone on with the body harness. It was now impossible for Pringles to get off.

I tried to leave the cone off as much as I could during the day, but had to keep an eye on Catty to make sure he wouldn't scratch his stitches, only using the body harness and cone when I had a client appointment and had to leave him on his own.

He was also harnessed and coned morning and late afternoon when I took him outside for a walk around the garden on the lead. At night, I used the cone with a soft collar - it seemed more comfortable for him to sleep in.

I felt so sorry for my poor cat.

Two weeks after the operation, I took Pringles - my one-eyed pirate - back to the Vet to have the sixteen stitches removed from his eyelids. There was still a lot of swelling, but it gradually subsided and the wound eventually healed. The eyebrow and fur where they'd shaved his little face before the operation started growing back, and his wound was becoming less noticeable.

It was still strange seeing him with only one eye. Pringles needed no adjustment period after the operation, and the vet doubted he was even aware that he'd lost the eye. She said the only thing he would notice was the absence of his daily headaches.

'Why are you winking at me?' Gary asked Pringles one evening.

I laughed. "It does look like he's winking."

Gary loves coming up with new nicknames for Pringles.

'I know, we can call him Winky,' he said.

'No, that's mean,' I chuckled. 'Please, don't.'

But Winky stuck.

A few weeks later Pringles was up to his old tricks; hiding away from me when it was time to lock him in for the night. Most days, Catty comes inside and puts himself to bed before the sun goes down, but there are odd days when he doesn't want to. He'll either hide under the house, somewhere in the garden, or he'll be visiting Murray and Joy and I'd have to get them to pass my "timeshare kitty" over the fence.

A few months back, the little rascal snuck into their house for a mid-afternoon visit. If their front door or kitchen door isn't open, he'll let himself in through any open window. After rubbing up and saying hello to everyone, Catty disappeared.

Sunset came and I thought Catty was in the garden. Murray and Joy thought he was home with me. As usual, they checked all the rooms in their house before closing the windows for the night, and hadn't seen Pringles anywhere.

Later that evening, Catty still hadn't come home. I called and called, searching the garden by torchlight, but couldn't find him anywhere. I sent a text to Joy asking if she could please check all their rooms once more, just in case he was hiding somewhere.

The little rascal had hidden in their computer room, curled up in a small space, so no one would see him. Needless to say, he was found and passed over the fence to sleep at home.

No sleepovers for naughty Catty.

14

Warning!

If you are reading this story to young children, or if you're sensitive and don't want to read about illness and death, please skip the next chapter and make your way to the photo section.

15

The Final Chapter

Pringles has been looking a little bloated these past few days, but how much seems to vary daily - some days he looks really puffy, the next he looks normal. At first I thought it might be gas as he's been drinking a lot of water, but something didn't feel right. I was sure my Catty was ill.

Pringles has a morning routine that occurs like clockwork every day: as soon as we unlock his cat flap, he runs down the back staircase, does his ablutions in the garden, and then hops over the fence to let himself into Murray and Joy's house to say "good morning," have kitty cuddles and cat snacks with them. Once done, he comes back home for his biscuits.

On Tuesday morning, he only nibbled at breakfast. Later that night I tried playing with him, but he only half-heartedly swatted at his toy. This was not normal. Usually he wiggles, pounces, bites, chews and kicks at his toy. Poor Catty looked very uncomfortable. I picked him up for a cuddle and he emitted a little squeaky meow.

'Sorry, my boy. Is your tummy sore?'

Thinking he might be having another bout of cystitis, I found some of his anti-inflammatory medication and gave him a dose. He settled down and fell asleep.

The next morning, I let him out, watching as he ran down the stairs. He only got halfway before he slowed and awkwardly hobbled down the last few steps. I was sure he was in pain, but this didn't stop him from jumping over the fence to go greet Murray and Joy, have cuddles and kitty treats.

My Catty is a creature of habit - mess one thing up in his little routine and his whole day is ruined.

I was worried. This hobble wasn't normal and my Catty looked very puffy around his middle. When he didn't come inside for breakfast, I went looking for him. I found him lying in his favourite spot at the bottom of the garden. He stayed there all morning, even after I'd tried to coax him inside with food and treats. This was completely out of character. At this time of day he'd usually have checked to see where I was, what I was doing, had a cuddle or scratch, and eaten some of his breakfast.

I phoned Whangaparāoa Vet Centre and managed to get an early afternoon appointment. I mentally prepared myself in case they needed to do blood tests and x-rays. I thought there might be a trapped hairball, or something he'd eaten in the garden that may have gotten stuck in his stomach. We were still in the first strict Level 4 Covid-19 lockdown, and I knew I'd have to drop Pringles off outside reception, not being allowed in with him during the consultation.

I arrived and phoned to let them know we were there. The receptionist asked me to leave Pringles in his cat carrier on the doorstep, and to return to my car, one of the vet nurses would come out in a gown, gloves and mask to collect him. I was to wait in the car for the vet to phone me once she'd checked him over.

Ten minutes ticked by ever so slowly. When the phone finally rang, I almost jumped out of my skin with fright.

'Hi Debbie, I've just checked over Pringles, and we're going to need to do blood tests and x-rays. I just need to get the go ahead from you,' Emma, the vet, said.

'It's fine. I thought you might need to do both.'

'We'll try do the tests while he's conscious as he's such a well-behaved cat. You can go home and I'll have someone phone when you can come collect him.'

Hanging up, I drove home. We live nearby, it's not even a ten minute drive. As I pulled into the driveway, my phone rang.

'I'm sorry to tell you this,' Emma said. 'It's not good news. I examined him and felt a lump in his abdomen. I thought it might be a tumour, so I called in another vet for a second opinion. She also suspects a tumour. Pringles seems to be in a lot of pain and won't let us touch his tummy to do a thorough examination. We need your approval to sedate him for x-rays. I'm afraid to say he's now grown horns and a pointy tail.'

I could just imagine Catty's claws and teeth lashing out everywhere. I gave my approval and waited for another call.

I sat down and cried. I'd lost my mom to cancer when I was 28, she was only 53, and now there was a possibility that I'd be losing my fur kid to this awful disease, too.

What will we do if he has cancer?

I paced around the lounge, waiting for Emma to call back. Half an hour later, my phone finally rang.

'The good news is that Pringles's internal organs are all functioning healthily: kidneys, liver, pancreas, et cetera. The bad news is he does have a tumour. It's on his liver and has grown onto his stomach. His blood tests have revealed a platelet level so low that we can't operate – his blood just won't clot.'

'Do you mind if I ask how low?'

'His platelet level is 5, it should be 150 or above.'

I was given the option of a referral to a specialist who would be able to tell me how big the tumour is, and how many lobes of Pringles's liver have been affected. The catch being that Pringles would need surgery, and before he can have an operation we'd need to get his platelet count up – poor Catty would need a full blood transfusion – and even then, there is no guarantee that this tumour is operable, or if he'd survive the operation.

My Catty is in pain and extremely ill.

Tears streaming down my face, I was trying hard not to sob over the phone as Emma continued.

'We need you to make a decision: do we wake him up from sedation and pump him full of fluids, so we can send him home for a day or two? It would leave him in an excruciating amount of pain and he'd have to be on steroids; or you can give us approval to euthanise him straight away, while he's still sedated.'

'Can I call you back in two minutes? I need to chat to my husband.'

'Of course, but we need an answer soon. We've only got ten minutes before the sedation starts to wear off.'

I hung up and sobbed.

It's too soon. It's not his time to leave me. I thought I'd still have at least another five years with him. He still looked healthy until yesterday.

I couldn't think straight, and I literally had seconds to make the most difficult decision of my life.

Do I get them to pump him full of steroids just so I can say goodbye, knowing he's in terrible pain? Or do I end his little life now, while he's unconscious? He won't even know anything has happened.

I told Gary what Emma had just said.

'He's your cat, you need to decide what you want.'

'Gary, I can't. I don't want Pringles to go. I want to say goodbye to him first,' I cried.

'Then tell them to put him on steroids.'

'It's selfish to keep him on steroids for a few days. He'll be in so much pain. How can I say goodbye like that, knowing I'm the one hurting him?'

I tried hard to compose myself before phoning Emma back.

'Please can you do it while he's still sedated,' I said quietly, trying not to sob down the line, knowing this must be just as terrible for her.

'Are you wanting him cremated or will you be burying him?' she asked softly.

'We're going to bury him,' I replied. 'Can I come say goodbye to him and be there when you give him the injection?'

'I'm terribly sorry, but we can't allow that. The level 4 lockdown doesn't allow us to let anyone into the clinic.'

I understood, but couldn't believe I wasn't going to get to see him one last time. My entire body shaking, I felt sick. As soon as I got off the phone with Emma, I dialled Murray and Joy's number. I had to tell them what was happening. I could see Joy standing in their office from our dining room window when she answered.

'Hi Joy,' I said. 'I have some bad news. I need you to sit down for this.'

'What's wrong, love,' she asked.

'Are you sitting down yet?' I asked, I could see she was still standing at the window, looking out over their back garden. I watched as she pulled the computer chair out and sat down. Once I knew she was seated, I told her what had just happened and that Pringles was being put to sleep while we spoke.

My Catty's life left his little body around 3pm, and Gary drove me to collect my precious bundle twenty minutes later. One of the nurses brought him out to the car, her eyes red, I know it must be hard for them, too. He'd been a 'patient' there for five years. Emma and the nurses had wrapped Catty in a little blanket before placing him in a white box with the words, "In loving memory of Pringles."

We took him home. Murray and Joy met us at the back fence to say goodbye to their "grand-fur kid" and little "Ratbag." I stroked Pringles's body and scratched his ears for the last time, his fur still warm, his face peaceful. It looked like he was sleeping.

We buried him in one of his favourite spots in the garden - at the end of the path between the planter boxes - underneath a white African Daisy, because he was an African pussy cat.

Pringles turned thirteen in February 2020. I think thirteen was his unlucky number.

It hurts me to think of how much pain he must have been in those last few months, especially the last two days.

I'm grateful for the time I got to spend with him the morning before he was put down. We sat in the sun while I brushed him, and afterwards, we sat together on the wooden bench, him in his favourite spot on the arm of the bench, me sitting on the seat next to him. We watched the birds and had a chat: I told him how I hoped he was a happy cat, how the 'kitty doctor' was going to make his sore tummy feel better, and how I was sorry that he wasn't feeling well.

I had no idea it would be the last time Catty and I would do this together. I thought I'd be bringing him home, and that we'd have a few more years together.

How does such a little being take up so much space? My heart and house feel empty. I can't believe how much this hurts.

I'm so sorry, Pringles.

My heart is broken.

My Catty is gone.

I hope he lived a happy life and knew how much I loved him. I miss him terribly. I like to think he's with my mom now, curled up on her lap instead of mine.

My Forever Pet

There's something missing in my home,
I feel it day and night,
I know it will take time and strength
before things feel quite right.

But just for now, I need to mourn,
My heart... it needs to mend.
Though some may say,
"It's just a pet,"
I know I've lost a friend.

You've brought such laughter to my home,
and richness to my days.
A constant friend through joy or loss
with gentle, loving ways.

Companion, friend, and confidante,
A friend I won't forget.
You'll live forever in my heart,
My sweet, forever pet.

\- Susanne Taylor

16

Photos

Baby Pringles - a pic from his adoption advert

Pringles' 2nd birthday

Smiling in his sleep

Playtime in the garden

The window he jumped from

Pringles, age 3 - October 2010

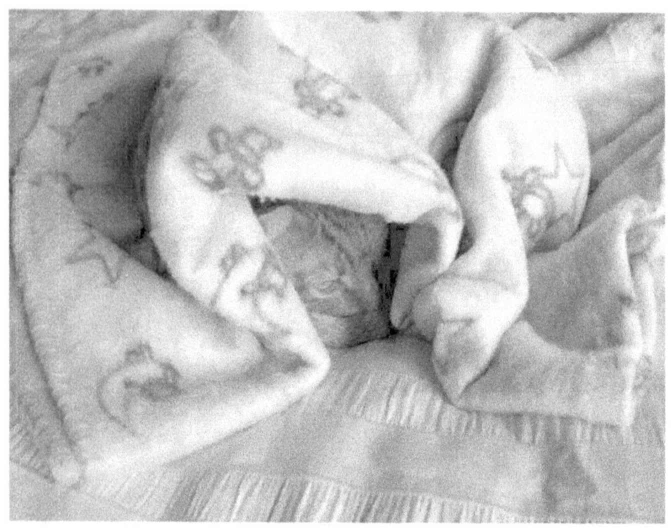

It's cold in New Zealand

Hide-'n-Seek ... He's not very good at hiding

A very sick Catty on my lap (Cat 'flu 2015)

Post-teeth cleaning 'selfie'
(shaved spot on his leg from the anaesthetic)

A garden of his own - Whangaparāoa, December 2015

Just chilling

A gift for me - banana peel

Favourite spot in front of the fire

Left eye turning dark
- age 9, Sept 2016

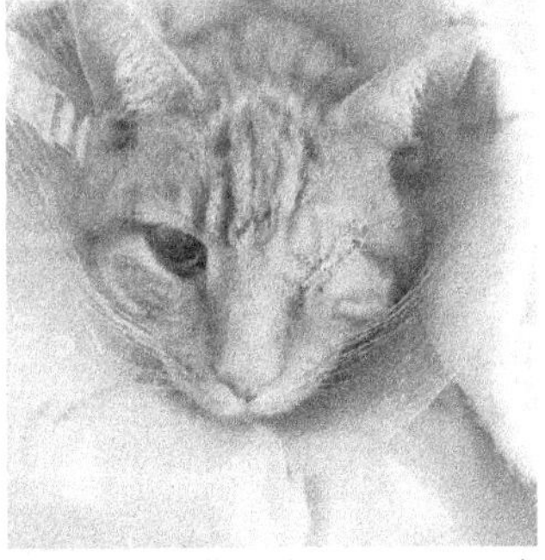

The night after his eye removal
surgery - June 2018

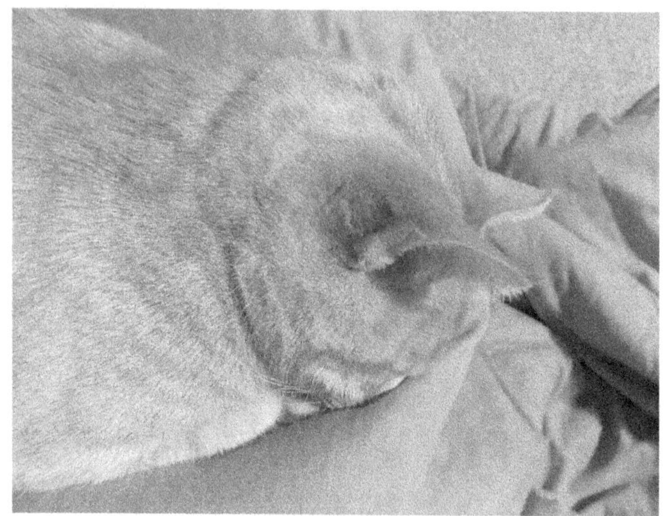

"I has a sad"
Pringles fast asleep on my lap

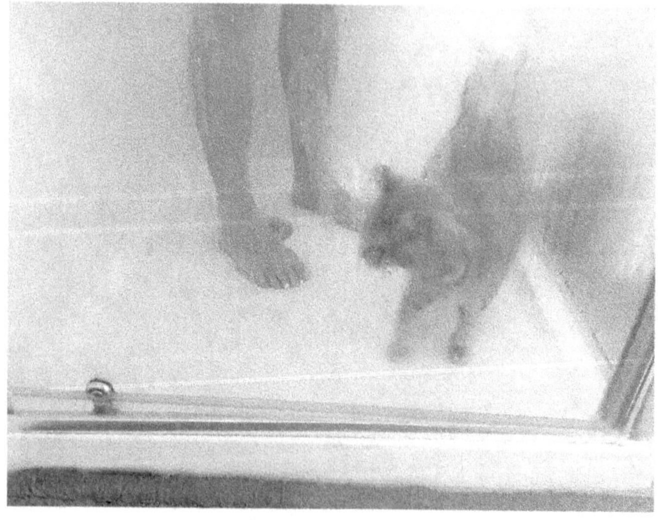

Pringles in the shower with Gary

Getting some fresh air after his eye operation (June 2018)

The bath mats are 'lava'

One-eyed pirate, also known as 'Winky'
- Pringles, age 10 (November 2018)

"If the birds can, why can't I?"
(November 2018)

Under the Christmas Tree
(December 2018)

Pringles broke the cat flap
(April 2020)

"Broken cat flap? It wasn't me." (April 2020)

Ready to jump on the couch - The last pic I took of him (April 2020)

"The Owl and the Pussycat"

Pringles' final resting place.
Buried under the white Africa Daisy.

Reviews Matter

Whether this story made you laugh or cry, please consider leaving an Amazon and/or Goodreads review.

Authors love reviews as much as they love writing, and they appreciate readers who leave honest reviews. Reviews help authors grow in more ways than you can imagine. It also helps new readers discover a self-published author who doesn't have the marketing budget of a big name on the bestseller list.

Help me get Pringles's story out there.
Thank you.
Debbie

About the Author

South African born, I moved to New Zealand in my mid-thirties.

Over the years I've written emails to family and friends, telling them about adventures on our travels, and a few kept urging me to take up writing, to convert my stories into books. It's only taken ten years, but I've finally started.

You can connect with me on:
- https://www.ramblingrose.co.nz
- https://www.facebook.com/ramblingrosenails
- https://www.instagram.com/ramblingrosenails

Also by Debbie Page-Wood

with fiction written under the pen name Amy Armitage.

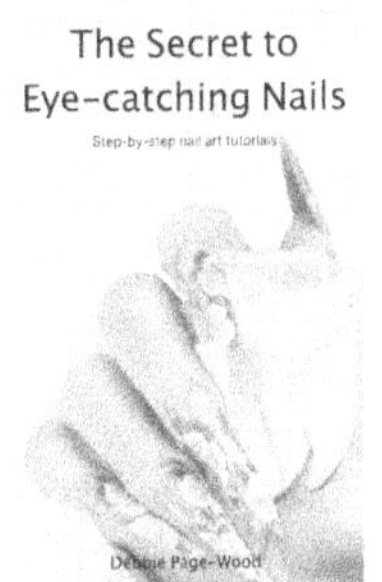

The Secret to Eye-catching Nails
Who doesn't love getting compliments on their nails from random strangers?

With tips, tricks, and step-by-step how-to guides, *The Secret to Eye Catching Nails* has 53 designs for you to learn from. Novices needn't worry, because the chapters flow from one into the other, using what was learned in the previous chapter to help create designs in the next, and most are really simple to recreate.

From understanding colour, colour schemes and mixing colours, to tools of the trade and various nail art mediums, this book covers it all. It includes working with pigments, chrome, creating ombré colour fades, various stamping techniques (as well as a few TikTok hacks), how to create different types of French manicures, how to use nail art foils, decals and glitter, as well as how to hand paint nail art. Debbie shares what she's learned from experience, in the hopes that it will help encourage novice and new graduate nail techs to think outside the box and do unexpected things on their own nail art journeys.

Kissing Frogs

Calling Emily's love life a disaster is the understatement of the year. She seems to attract 'bad boys', and so far they've all been just that ... bad. She soon discovers that there are some pretty ugly toads in this bog of frogs that she has to navigate on her quest to find 'The One'. In hindsight, some of them should have been sidestepped or completely stepped over instead of her falling for their charms.

From chance meetings, dealing with fetishes, bondage, being cheated on and so much more, Emily's been there, done that, and kissed a lot of frogs along the way. Sadly, not all frogs turn into princes, some will forever remain toads. But how much does one girl have to go through before finally finding her prince?

Kissing Frogs is not your typical 'boy meets girl, fall in love, and get married' romance - it's more than that. So much more. It's a tale of how parents' actions and attitudes affect their children in more ways than they realise. It's a journey of self-discovery, self-acceptance, and finally, self-love. Emily's story begins with a teenage crush and spans over the next decade on her quest to find 'The One'.

If you've ever felt unheard or misunderstood, blamed yourself or thought that there may be something wrong with you because past relationships failed, or wondered why you ever dated one of your exes, then *Kissing Frogs* may enlighten you.

TRIGGERS / MILD SPOILER WARNING: This sexy, coming-of-age, non-traditional romance contains graphic discussions and scenes that include mental health issues, substance abuse, profanity, fetishes, sex, abuse, views on abortion and religion.

89

Not recommended for readers under the age of 18.